MW01230544

Dog Jokes

Funny Jokes for Dog Lovers

Aaron Stark

Dog Jokes: Funny Jokes for Dog Lovers

Copyright © 2019 by Aaron Stark

D J M 3 5 7 2 1 1

DOG JOKES

What do dogs do after they've been dating their girlfriend for a while? *They Jack Russel Marrier.*

What trick did ancient Greeks teach their dogs? *The Achilles Heel.*

Why don't dalmatians make good ninjas? *They're always spotted.*

What dog keeps things longer than they should? *A hoarder-collie.*

Why didn't the dog use its vacation time? *He was told it would rollover.*

What's the best hiking trail for a dog? *The Appalachian ridgeback.*

What type of dog would be good in a fight? *A boxer.*

What did the dog say when its boss asked her to stay late? *Gnaw.*

What type of dog studies in England? *A Yorkshire terrier.*

What does a dog use when it's hot? *A dober-fan.*

Why did the poodle vote for the Green party? *They always cheer for the underdog.*

What does a dogs say when their owners get married? *I now pawnounce you man and woof.*

Why did the mutt want a manual car? *It wanted a mixed speed.*

What did the dog playing poker say? *Are you gonna call my ruff?*

What kind of dog would you call to fix your toilet? *A Plummer Terrier.*

Who do dogs call when they need to fix a sink? *The faucet hound.*

What's a dog's favorite Thai food? *Panang Kuri.*

What would dogs sing around a campfire? *Combai-yah.*

What would kind of dog would 3 Little Pigs own? *A Japanese Chinny Chin Chin.*

Why did the dog join the ringette team? *She was a skate-dane.*

What kind of dog makes the best cheerleader? *A pom-pomeranian.*

What does a dog say when the door won't close? *Komondor.*

What do prosecutors do when they charge a dog with a crime? *Show the burden of woof.*

What kind of speakers would you use in a kennel? *Subwoofers.*

What would a dog say to their friend who won't go in the water? *Dunker.*

How does a dog make a sandwich? *With pure bread.*

What do dachshunds eat for dinner? *Dog food. What do you think I was going to say, hot dogs?*

What kind of dog only watches romantic comedies? *A rom-com-eranian.*

What kind of dessert is made for dogs? *A Poodle Strudel.*

What's a dog's favorite type of rum? *Picardy.*

How did the dog get separated from the group? *I'm not sure, he must've strayed away*

Why would a dog go on a tropical vacation? *To get a dober-tan.*

Why couldn't the dog speak French? *It was a Grand Anglo-phone.*

What do you respond when your dog asks you to pick it up from the airport? *Kai Ken't.*

What breed of dog makes a great lion tamer? *A Whippet.*

Why was the dog excited ready for the end of school dance? *She was a prom-eranian.*

What did the dog name his bakery? *Need for Breed.*

What did the dog bring to the potluck? *A kennel salad.*

What do dogs sing at sports events? *The Karakachant.*

Why did the dog get fired from their job? *He was a late-dane.*

What did the dog say to its parents when they said it had to go to the park alone? *Cantabrian a friend?*

If a dog was in Jurassic Park, what would it say to the raptors? *Drever, girl.*

What do old dogs play in the nursing home? *Dingo!*

What kind of dog is always making mischievous plans? *A Portuguese plotter dog.*

What did the dog get when it was 2 under par in golf? *A beagle.*

What boardgame do dogs get lost in? *Jonangi.*

What did the dog's neighbors say when he was playing music too loud? *"Hey, buddy can you muzzle the sound?"*

How do poodles get their food taken away? *In doggie-bags.*

What is a dog's favorite soup?
Shiba Instew.

Why do a lot of dogs go into chemistry and biology? *They like doing lab reports.*

What waterpark would a dog go to? *Calupsoh.*

What did the dog living in the woods say? *"I'm really ruffing it."*

What type of dog makes the best governor? *A state-dane.*

What do you call a dog who gets sick a lot? *A Bersneeze Mountain Dog.*

What did mama dog say to papa dog when the puppy wouldn't cross the river? *"Maybe just Jack Russell Carrier."*

What do you call a dog with bright yellow hair? *A blond-erainian.*

What type of dog gets a lot of gifts at Christmas? *A Border-Jolly.*

What kind of dog likes to shred cheese? *A grate-dane.*

Which sorority would a dog be in? *Alpha Phido.*

What kind of dog would you hire as a lawyer? *A debate-dane.*

Where do dogs make great restaurant critics? *They like to yelp.*

What did they call the collie that jumped over another collie? *A leap-dog.*

What kind of walk do dogs go on? *A boerstrole.*

What do dog's like to bake with? *Jindough.*

What do dogs drink on a hot day? *Koolie-aid.*

What do you call an art piece your dog makes? *A labradoodle.*

What do you call two dogs cuddling? *Capoodling.*

Why was the dog allowed in the bank? *It had a white collar.*

What type of dog does Dracula own? *A bloodhound.*

What do you call a dog that needs to go on a diet? *An over-weight-dane.*

What's a dog's favorite type of transportation? *The Greyhound.*

What concert did the dog attend? *The Waggo Tango.*

What kind of dog would star in Wonder Woman? *Galgo-dot.*

What's a dog's favorite word to use in an essay? *Fur-thermore.*

What would a dog-friendly pirate ship use to battle another ship? *Canaans.*

What do you call a dog with a camera? *A photografur.*

What did the dog's parents tell the puppy to do about her school bully? *Pinscher and he'll back off.*

How did the dalmatian get into the sold-out show? *Someone saved it a spot.*

What would you call a dog serving alcohol? *A bark-keeper.*

What do dogs build with blankets? *Hovaforts.*

What do you say when your friend Jack asks to have your dog? *I'm Tornjak.*

What's the happiest type of dog? *A Corglee.*

What kind of dog would you want in a band? *A rocker spaniel.*

How are there so many dogs on Earth? *I don't know, It's mind-beagling.*

Why did the dog get a job at Fed-Ex? *He wanted to be a freight-dane.*

What does a dog cook eggs on? *A dober-pan.*

What do you call a dog in a bog? *Mudi.*

What kind of dog do pirates bring when searching for buried treasure? *A golden retriever.*

What is a dog's favorite Journey song? *Don't Stop Retrievin'.*

What dog would be on Grey's Anatomy? *Keeshonda Rhimes.*

What do you tell a dog when there's a rabbit infestation? *Huntaway.*

What do hungry dogs eat for breakfast? *A great Danish.*

What kind of dog never wins a race? *A Sloughi.*

What is Queen's University's unofficial mascot? *The Serbian Tricolor Hound.*

What breed of dog has the world record for lifting weights? *The Jacked Muscle Terrier.*

How did the dog feel when it did a trick but didn't get a treat? *Ticked off.*

Why did the dentist get a dog? *He liked spending time with canines.*

What do you call a wager made between two dogs at a pub? *A barbet.*

What do you tell your dog when it's looking for its shoes and you see some cubbies? *Pekingese.*

What's a dog's favorite Aqua song? *Dr. Bones.*

What does a dog get after a night out of partying? *A Hanover.*

What kind of dog would you play volleyball with? *A blocker spaniel.*

What dog works the hardest? *A jack hustle terrier.*

What's a dog's writing utensil of choice? *A Shar Pei.*

Where do dogs like to sit on a farm? *On the back pooch.*

What kind of dog would a baker own? *A Siberian bread-dog.*

What would a dog make a canoe out of? *Birch bark.*

How did the dog injure itself? *It Braque its back.*

Why did the young dog want a new career in business? *It wanted to be a yuppie dog.*

When you trade a crumb with a dog to land a plane.
Kromfohrlander.

What type of dog goes bad the fastest? *A rott-weiler.*

What did Aladdin name his dog?
Diamond in the Ruff.

What do you do when dogs are trying to break into the house? *Make a Jack Russel Barrier.*

What dog do you use to find your lost poodle? *A Pudelpointer.*

What kind of dog comes from a caterpillar? *A Papillon.*

What do you tell your bed-hog dog? *Give me back the Kuvasz.*

Why don't you ever see an Australian Shepperd working at a minimum wage job? *They don't like working re-tail.*

Why did the dog buy a new car? *She wanted a sun-woof.*

What dog would bully you on the playground? *A mocker spaniel.*

Where do dogs work at a shopping mall? *The infurmation desk.*

Why did the dog put its fur on the walls? *It was told it needed another coat.*

What would a dog say when you ask if it would rather beef or chicken? *It's a Tosa-p.*

What kind of dog is great at reading tarot cards? *A fate-dane.*

What does a dog say when it gets a Sphynx for its birthday? *Harrier.*

What does your dog say after you won't stop irritating it? *"God, I'm so Samoyed."*

What does a magician say when it pulls a dog out of its hat? *Abra-ka-labradora.*

Which dog breed is guaranteed to get into heaven? *The Saint Bernard.*

What does your dog say when your pencils are dull? *Schapendoes.*

What sport do dogs like to play? *Collie-ball.*

Why do dogs like the rain? *When it rains you get a lot of poodles.*

Why do dogs own a lot of house plants? *So they don't have to go outside when it rains.*

What do you always have to ask a forgetful dog? *Don't you Maremma?*

How would a dog greet you in Italian? *Ciao-Ciao.*

What type of dog asks the most questions in school? *A Chi-why-why?*

What did the landlord tell its canine tenants when it wanted to evict them? *Sorry, your leash is up.*

Why did the dog have to use Head and Shoulders? *It had dandrufff.*

Why didn't the dog answer the phone? *It didn't have collar ID.*

What do dogs eat for Sunday brunch? *Pawcakes.*

What did the dog say to the ghost? *Are you fur-real?*

What did the dog say when its owner took away its treats? *I'm fur-ious.*

What does a police dog wear for protection? *A bullet-woof vest.*

What did the aggressive dog receive playing basketball? *A technical growl.*

What did the hound reply when asked to clean its room? *"Borzwhyyyyyy?"*

What did the dog say when its friend asked him to steal a hotdog? *"We dachshouldn'td do that."*

What happens when two dogs get in a fight? *They mutt heads.*

What do you tell a dog that only showers once a month? *Improve your Hygen.*

How did the dog get out of jail? *He filed for pawrole.*

What did the dog say to its friend who disobeyed direct orders? *"You went dogue."*

What do you tell your friend Ken when he asks why your dog is licking his face? *He wants to Kishu Ken!*

What did the dog receive after graduating university? *It's pedegree.*

What kind of chocolate would a dog eat if they could? *A Malteser.*

What do dogs put on toast? *Dober-jam.*

What did the dogs say when they'd decorated their home? *It's fully fur-nished.*

How do dogs get their kids to soccer practice? *In the dober-van.*

Why did the dog go on an adventure? *She wanted to em-bark on something new.*

What did Homer Simpson name their new dog? *Fi-Doh!*

Why did the dog cross the road? *It thought the chicken was a ball.*

What kind of dogs like to work in coal mines? *The ones with blue collars.*

Why did the collie wake up late? *She had a ruff night.*

What do they serve at Canine Thanksgiving? *German Shephard's Pie.*

What do dogs do to the television when they get a phone call? *They malamute it.*

What is the most fragile type of dog? *A Porcelaine.*

What's the best type of dog to guard a fence? *A gate-dane.*

What's a dog's favorite kitchen tool? *A potato heeler.*

What type of dog would you find at a casino? *A blue dealer.*

What dog could star in high school musical? *Shar Pei Evans.*

How do dogs stay warm? *They use a fur-nace.*

How did the dog get across the pond? *It swam-eranian.*

What do you call two dogs working together? *A co-lab-oration.*

What happens to a dog's fur in the humidity? *It gets Bichon Frizzy.*

What do dog's order at the bakery? *A poppyseed beagle.*

What toy would a dog use to play with a cat? *A laser Pointer.*

What kind of e-mail virus would your dog send you? *Dober-spam.*

What kind of dog would be great at volleyball? *An English Setter.*

What do dogs like to eat at movies? *Pupcorn.*

What is the luckiest type of dog? *An Irish wolfhound.*

What do you call a dog that's been in the water for too long? *An English prune-hound.*

How would a dog keep water in a bath? *With a pug.*

What type of pasta do dogs eat? *Bolognese*.

What dog would be in the Rolling Stones? *Mick Jagdterrier.*

What do dog's say when you pull their leash too hard? *Hokkaidon't.*

What would a dog have at a fast food restaurant? A *Berger*.

What kind of dog would be in Lord of the Rings? *Shbeagle.*

What did the dog say when the judge asked him why he turned to a life of crime? *"I didn't choose the pug life, the pug life chose me."*

What do you tell your parents when you bring home 10 dogs? *"They retrieve gold, I did this for our family."*

What breed of dog smells like an old carpet? *The Siberian Musky.*

What kind of dog is made for a band on the road? *A tour bred.*

How does a dog raise something high off the ground? *With a Puli.*

What's a dog's favorite city? *Frank-fur-t.*

What did the dog lawyer use to help with his research? *A parabeagle.*

What candy would you give a cute dog? *A collie-pop.*

What kind of dog likes to snapchat? *A recorder-collie.*

What do you tell a dog with a big nose? *You have a Giant Schnauz.*

What did one dog tell their sad friend? *You're pawfect.*

What did a dog reply when asked to sing on the spot? *Alright, I'll mast-riff.*

How did the dog make it home so fast? *He dober-ran the entire way.*

Why did the new mom dog get a ticket? *She was littering.*

What's a dog's favorite cereal?
Mini-Wheatens.

Why don't dogs ever buy anything
with cash in the United Kingdom?
They don't like using pounds.

What do you call an electrocuted
dog? *A shocker spaniel.*

What did the witch dog say to
someone who scorned her?
Cursinu.

What's a dog's favorite order at McDonnalds? *The McNab.*

How would you compliment a dog's sneaky smarts? *Call it Kunming.*

What did the shoe vendor tell the dog? *You want a pyrenees?*

Why did the hound get promoted? *They found her skills to be multi-basseted.*

Why didn't the dog complain when there was a fly in her soup? *She didn't want to ruffffle any feathers.*

Where kind of shoes do dogs wear? *Hush puppies.*

Where would a dog keep a car? *A barking lot.*

What did one dog tell another to express its love? *"Phalene for you."*

Where does a dog go to get snacks? *The Vendeen Machine.*

What's a dog's favorite singer? *Tom Bones.*

What type of fish do dog's like in the topics? *A Barra-Kutta.*

What breed of dog would be in Beauty and the Beast? *Gascon.*

What did the doctor say to her kids holding a chew toy? *Get it to the Lab.*

Why didn't the dog bring its water bowl? *She furgot.*

What would dog aliens say when they come to earth? *Cretans, Earthlings.*

What do dogs order at the coffee shop? *A Pugkin Spice Latte.*

What kind of dog likes to keep its feet warm? *A socks-hound.*

What type of dog will infest your home and eat your cheese? *A Rat Terrier.*

One day a dog woke up and discovered she didn't fit into her favorite sweater anymore. *She said, "I need to go on a diet, I'm getting a little husky."*

What do you call a tiny dog that's not very happy? *A little melancholy.*

What do dog waiters say giving out hors d'oeuvres? *Havacheese.*

Why did the dog work at a collection agency? *He was good at people for hounding for money.*

What did the dog reply when greeted in England? *"Elo."*

Where do dogs perform musicals? *Broadstray.*

What did the girl dog tell the boy dog when he couldn't decide whether to date her? *You're such a Maltease.*

What dog likes to relax? *A calm-eranian.*

What's a dog's favorite AC/DC song? *Chinook Me All Night Long.*

What do you call a dog that cries all day? *A chi-wah-wah.*

What do dogs order at 7/11? *Slush puppies.*

Why don't you ever see a dog working in a factory? *They don't like union poos.*

What should you do if your dog eats your shoes? *Buy him his own pair.*

Made in the USA
Columbia, SC
18 March 2020